Nothing Else Matters

Words and Music by
James Hetfield and Lars Ulrich

4

Never cared for what they do. Never cared for what they

know, oh, but I know.

So close, no matter how far. Couldn't be much more from the heart.

Forever trusting who we are. And nothing else matters.

Never cared for what they do. Never cared for what they

know, oh, but I know.

I nev-er o-pened my-self this way.____

Life is ours, we live it

our way.____

All these words I don't just say.____